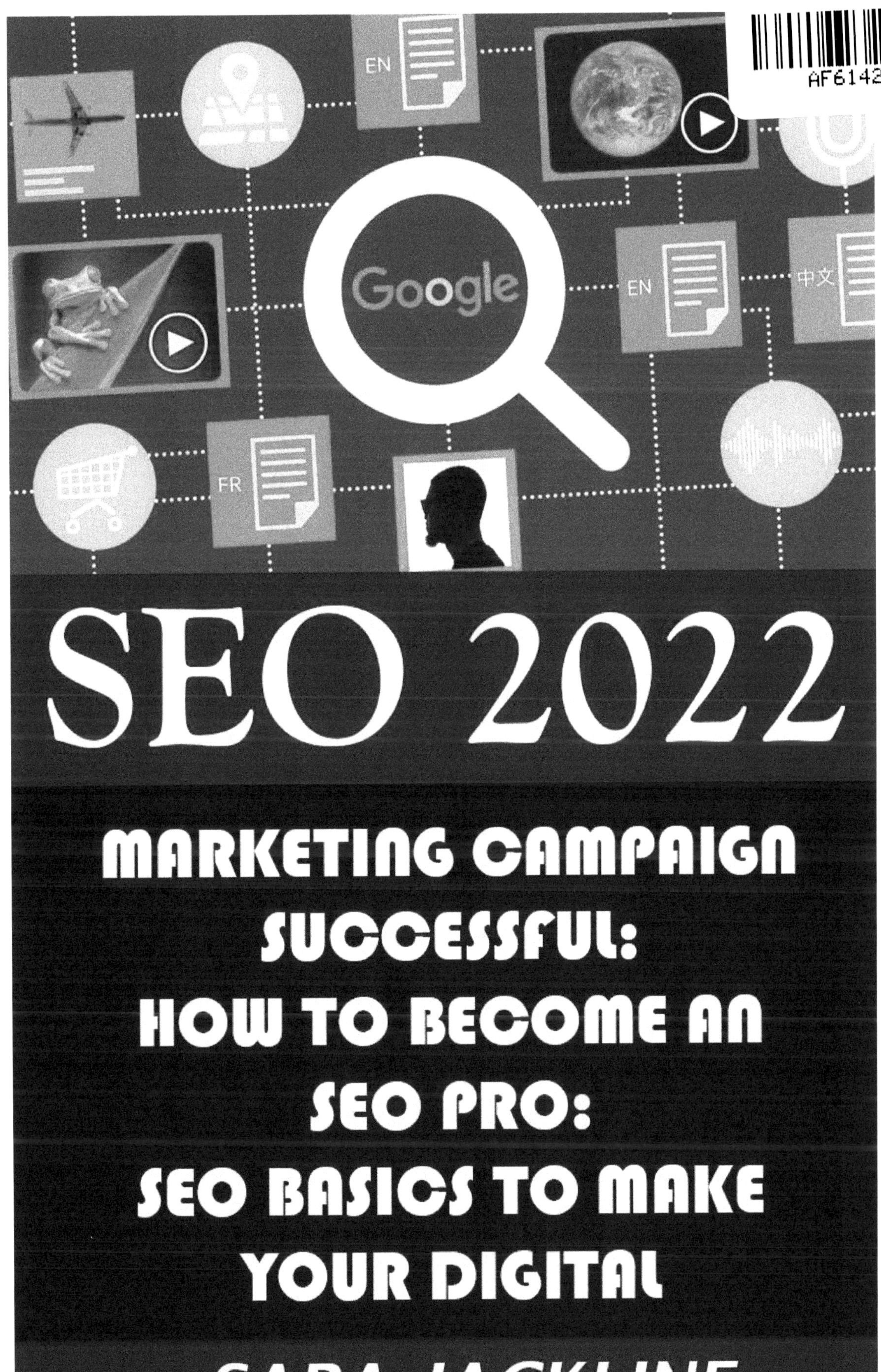

EN
Google
EN
中文
FR
SEO 2022
MARKETING CAMPAIGN
SUCCESSFUL:
HOW TO BECOME AN
SEO PRO:
SEO BASICS TO MAKE
YOUR DIGITAL
SARA JACKLINE

SEO 2022: Marketing Campaign Successful: How To Become An SEO Pro: SEO Basics To Make Your Digital

Introduction

search engine optimization or application optimization isn't always rocket science. It takes little attempt to grasp the topic. After getting educated in search engine optimization, a applicable expert can count on an awesome month-to-month income. maximum significantly, throughout the planet, new ventures are floated each now, and then, there is a demand for application optimization and this call for is continual implying that there is no dearth of jobs in the course of this field.

This weblog specializes in the diverse approaches wherein an character can make use of to emerge as an search engine optimization expert.

How To Become An SEO Professional

Tips for Becoming an inquiry Engine Optimisation Professional

Following are some of the thoughts of turning into an search engine optimization expert:-

Visiting an Expert

If you are a novice to search engine optimization you then definately do now no longer want to worry. Instead, go to an professional and start mastering the hints associated with the subject. If the professional perhaps a chum of yours then you may get reductions on schooling. After the pinnacle of the schooling, after you emerge as assured of the subject, you may observe for jobs with multinational agencies or non-public restricted agencies as a fresher.

By Taking Online Lessons

There are many web sites to be had on-line that deliver capability inexperienced persons appropriate schooling on the subject. If you would really like to discover search engine optimization all with the aid of using your self you then definately would really like to require on-line training the usage of appropriate on-line tutorials.

There are tutorials to be had in an effort to offer in-intensity expertise approximately on-web page additionally as off-web page optimization.

Join an search engine optimization Firm

Yet every other factor which you actually can do if you have got appropriate conversation capabilities is to join an search engine optimization organization as a fresher. While you work you would really like to be smart sufficient to take role sources in the course of a way so as which you study the thoughts and hints of the subject.

If you find out which you actually are assured approximately the subject then you may maintain with an equal organisation in any other case you may flow to a much higher role after a while . in the course of this context, it is vital to say that almost all agencies decide upon experienced

search engine optimization experts and hence if you may display paintings revel in for your CV along applicable capabilities then you will be in outstanding call for amongst capability employers.

Visit Social Media Websites

You can go to social media web sites like Facebook, LinkedIn, and reap possibilities to discover search engine optimization. The social media web sites additionally offer process possibilities to applicants who're professional inside the subject.

Off-Page Optimization is simple While On-Page can be a Bit Involved

If you are an search engine optimization expert you then definately need to don't forget the very truth that the subject is regularly categorized below sorts 1) On-Page Optimization 2)

Off-web page Optimization. in the course of this context, it is applicable to function that Off-web page optimization is relatively clean in comparison to On-web page optimization tasks. There are many agencies that offer Off-web page optimization paintings to process seekers.

So, there may be no dearth of software optimization paintings.

However, if you may do On-web page paintings along Off-web page paintings you then definately're some of the professionals then you will be in outstanding call for amongst virtual advertising and marketing agencies in search of search engine optimization services.

This weblog discusses the numerous methods with the aid of using which an man or woman can get educated in software optimization. It additionally discusses the paintings possibilities as a long way as virtual advertising and marketing cares .

SEO Basics To Make Your Digital Marketing Campaign Successful

search engine marketing is that the abbreviation of application Optimisation. it is all approximately mastering and the usage of tactics, techniques to enhance the visibility of internet sources like websites, webweb sites in numerous application effects pages. If you are an search engine marketing govt you then definately would love to own the basics proper to acquire achievement to your virtual advertising and marketing campaign. This weblog discusses the search engine marketing fundamentals which can be useful to your for the expert application optimizer.

Understand What the clients Are seeking to find

It is to understand that as a informed search engine marketing govt it is very tough to your component to optimize a web webweb page with out know-how what the clients are seeking to find. You as an inquiry engine optimizer were given to apply feel to training session what your clients are checking out.

You want to paste to the following factors to understand what your clients are searching for:

Try finding out the most famous technique all through which humans search for your business.

Comprehend different approaches humans search for an equal component using a application.

Emphasize long-tail key phrases whilst trying to find using a application.

Do granular searches greater constant with the needs of the clients.

Search For famous additionally as enticing subjects to your subject and write content material on the ones subjects.

Try increasing your key-word list.

To acquire achievement in application optimization you would love to require into attention humans's perspectives some specific subjects or niche. you would love to discuss the problems that the humans face. you would love to talk to the clients and decide the language that they may be the usage of.

Following are some of the crucial approaches via way of means of which you will turn out to be a hit in application optimization:-

Post in Forums

Do key-word studies and evaluation

Comprehend the metrics which can be in the back of the centered key phrases. These metrics may also consist of key-word difficulty, seek volume, area authority, web page authority, key-word competitiveness.

To do key-word studies and evaluation it is recommended which you absolutely create an excel sheet, spotlight the metrics which you absolutely are the usage of, populate the respective metric's subject with values as in opposition to the key-word which you absolutely are the usage of.

Create Webpages which can be optimized for searches

Focus on On-Page Optimisation

Keyword studies and evaluation is that the initiative to attract in natural visitors in your business. Next, concentrate on on-web page optimization all through a virtual advertising and marketing campaign. If you are using a Word Press internet site then it is advocated which you absolutely set up suitable plugins to your internet site. Create on-web page content material that is applicable in your business.

all through this context, it is applicable to function that there are 3 kinds of searches and that they're navigational, informational, and transactional. For greater in this go to applicable sources to be had online.

Following are some of the thoughts to concentrate on on-web page optimization:-

Use brief and descriptive URLs

Create compelling meta titles additionally as descriptions

Use headers additionally as sub-headers to make a logical structure

Focus on optimizing your images

Lay emphasis on solving a schema

Other Aspects that Help to shape You a much higher application Optimizer

Make your Website reachable to human beings additionally as seek engines. affirm that your internet portal masses promptly. specialize in putting in an SSL certificate. specialize in developing a domain map to your internet site. apart from these, there are numerous different components of virtual advertising and marketing that allows to enhance this system optimization abilities of the expert internet marketer.

Understanding The Significance - Content Writing In SEO

search engine marketing or application optimization is extraordinarily crucial for the enlargement of a commercial enterprise. Web entrepreneurs or search engine marketing experts who're accountable for doing this system optimization of purchaser web sites require adopting search engine marketing techniques to boost the visibility of the net webweb page inside the numerous application outcomes pages. the net webweb page visibility relies upon on how properly the search engine marketing professional conducts on-web page additionally as off-web page optimization of the purchaser internet site. inside the context of on-web page or off-web page application optimization, it is crucial to recognize that the pressure is commonly at the net webweb page contents. it is crucial that the content material for on-web page additionally as off-web page application optimization is properly written with right distribution of key phrases, anchor textual content. the goal is to attract in an increasing number of net visitors to a commercial enterprise. From this angle, the significance of content material writing and content material writers is excessive whilst it includes application optimization.

Tips on Writing search engine marketing Contents

This weblog discusses the way you should write content material even as doing on-web page or off-web page search engine marketing sports.

On-Page Content Writing

in case you are focussing on on-web page sports you then definately apprehend which you genuinely want to put in writing extremely good content material on your internet site pages. the goal is to attract in an increasing number of visitors for your commercial enterprise. Understand that extra visitors implies better lead-era and eventually extra conversion of outcomes in sales. While writing on-web page content material similar to the content material for a internet site's approximately-us web page, you want to be very unique approximately your commercial enterprise, you want to highlight your commercial enterprise objective. While writing the content material you may use anchor textual content as and in which required. The hyperlinks which you genuinely use were given to be applicable. There should not be overuse of key phrases. The key-word distribution should not exceed 1%-3% inside the whole content material. If you comply with those regulations you then definately find out that your internet site content material is presentable and draws an increasing number of on line visitors.

Off-web page Content Writing

Off-web page application optimization way hyperlink constructing. Link constructing in search engine marketing is extraordinarily crucial as it enables to boost the web page rank of a web webweb page, it enables to boost the DA or area authority price, the PA, or web page authority price of a web webweb page. During the approach of hyperlink constructing, the net entrepreneurs require to submit content material along applicable hyperlinks in the course of some of weblog sites, article sites, discussion board sites, query solutions webweb page,

handout sites. to make the content material the net entrepreneurs require the participation of content material writers. to attempt to off-web page content material writing the net entrepreneurs require to comply with a few regulations. They require to put in writing down content material at the subject, consist of key phrases which are applicable to the subject. The content material writers require to apply anchor texts linking applicable web sites or net resources. in the course of this context, it is applicable to function that the content material writers can do key-word studies to are trying to find out the key phrases for use for the content material, alternatively, the listing of key phrases goes to be supplied via way of means of the purchaser. There should not be an overuse of the key phrases.

the entire content material have to have a key-word density inside the variety of 1% to 3 only.

This weblog highlights the very reality that content material writing is immensely crucial for each on-web page additionally as off-web page search engine marketing. Therefore, next time you would really like to attempt to to search engine marketing of your purchaser's internet site then make sure to hire the same old offerings of informed content material writer.

Changing The Way You Expand: View Your Business

Nowadays, application optimization has turn out to be a gold mine for various on line marketers. it is turn out to be enterprise-driven, and nobody does it for leisure. The search engine marketing specialists are incredibly professional of their activity and with a have a take a observe your internet site, they are going to apprehend what have to be fixed. As those specialists paintings on diverse search engine marketing offerings and optimize severa web sites, they want the revel in to discern for this enterprise. that is regularly why you would really like to lease a dependable search engine marketing business enterprise in Gurgaon.

Why does one Need search engine marketing in your Website?

If you're a enterprise proprietor however don't have any clue approximately search engine marketing techniques that operate, it is crucial to lease an search engine marketing agency. they are going to carry out heaps of studies earlier than providing your appropriate techniques and answers in your enterprise expansion. With the right specialists, you may get a higher rating spot on Google, and your brands' internet site can get extra natural site visitors and capability customers.

A well-educated professional makes use of diverse techniques and eventually, exceptional capabilities to manipulate exceptional web sites and accumulate the desired results. They recognise what will make a web webweb page and what goes to interrupt it.

With well-designed search engine marketing Services in Gurgaon, you may construct a sturdy consumer dating also. Moreover, you would really like search engine marketing to get leads and flourish your enterprise inside the on line market.

To make your internet site attain the very best of the quest rating, you would really like right techniques made via way of means of specialists as each characteristic that is going into your internet site have to be dependable sufficient to shape your internet site outshine your competition.

Benefits of Hiring a Trusted search engine marketing Company

search engine marketing offerings are regularly custom designed as in line with your enterprise desires and budget. There are numerous advantages of search engine marketing offerings and using search engine marketing offerings. These specialists can help your enterprise to reach new heights.

search engine marketing Enhances your Website: search engine marketing is giant in your enterprise internet site as nearly each enterprise faces competition.

it is had to assist agencies to reach capability leads and clients. An search engine marketing offerings business enterprise in Gurgaon will manual you in imposing the techniques which might be crucial for enhancing your visibility inside the searches and improving your possibilities to reach potential customers.

Get Different Set of Expert Eyes: Permitting an search engine marketing professional to appear at your enterprise and formulate exceptional advertising and marketing techniques will make certain that your enterprise expands to a exceptional level. it is due to the fact search engine marketing specialists will view your enterprise from the consumer's factor of view and might make certain that your internet site draws traffic and promotes your services and products effectively. affirm to determine a relied on search engine marketing business enterprise in Gurgaon to keep away from enterprise failures.

No Investment in search engine marketing Tools & Skills: As search engine marketing can be a dynamic field, it continues on changing, and agencies have to adhere to the ones changes. With a dependable professional, you do now no longer get to put money into mentoring your search engine marketing crew or shopping for crucial search engine marketing equipment. They already have the equipment and educate their search engine marketing professionals due to the fact it's their top enterprise.

A Look At The Important Qualities Of Professional SEO

For on-line PR offerings, search engine optimization blogs and articles are immensely essential. Besides search engine optimization blogs and articles are critical for social media control offerings. a vital a part of off-web page search engine optimization is link-building. By often posting clean content material on a topic along hyperlinks to company web sites allows a enterprise to attract in increasingly more customers to the brand. When speaking approximately posting clean contents it manner the professional author has were given to jot down the blogs or articles. it is advised, that for writing tasks, a enterprise ought to are seeking the information of a skilled search engine optimization content material author.

This weblog is an attempt to understand the abilities that a informed search engine optimization weblog writers ought to use to jot down down stuff for a enterprise or brand.

Qualities of informed search engine optimization Content Writer

Following are a pair of factors approximately search engine optimization weblog writing that informed search engine optimization article author ought to use at the same time as writing contents:-

Do Adequate Research on Keywords

search engine optimization contents are significantly hooked into the usage of key phrases. Therefore, at the same time as writing blogs or articles you need to do considerable key-word research. you would love to apply the maximum key-word as soon as in the title, as soon as in the introduction,

as soon as throughout a subheading, as soon as in the fundamental frame of a 500 worded content material. While the use of key phrases verify which you sincerely keep away from key-word stuffing.

Use Keywords Appropriately

Try to apply the maximum key-word in the content material throughout a way just so the key-word density is a smaller quantity than 3%. other than the use of the maximum key-word attempt the use of associative key phrases in the write-up. Avoid key-word stuffing. Use long-tail key phrases if required. Use latent semantic indexing key phrases if needed.

Write Contents About Stuffs that parents appearance after

If you are writing a bit of writing or weblog on a topic then apprehend that the selection of the situation ought to be such it draws the readers. The contents ought to be written on subjects that parents appearance after. Understand that if increasingly more readers examine your write-up then it is able to assist your enterprise to expand.

Understand the fundamentals of Technical search engine optimization

While writing search engine optimization stuffs it is essential to recognize how Google crawls sites. Keeping these items into attention you must write content material. There are different essential fundamentals of technical search engine optimization which you sincerely can get to apprehend in case you browse applicable on-line subjects.

Make the Content Long and Attractive

It is discouraged to live your weblog or article short. If you are writing a weblog or a bit of writing then try and restrict the content material inside seven hundred words. Use key phrases in the content material accurately and make it appealing to the readers.

Watch Out The Analytics

Mere content material writing may not help you in getting the desired audience. you would love to try and to the search engine optimization element nicely with the content material. More importantly,

you would love to study out for the analytics additionally to come to be a hit with search engine optimization weblog writing.

Edit Work On Requirements

One of the most essential elements of search engine optimization content material writing is to edit paintings now then.

The paintings ought to be edited preserving because of the content material necessities for enterprise purposes.

Share the Content Once it is Posted Online

After having written search engine optimization content material you need to put up and proportion the content material on-line.

Understand That Practice Makes One Perfect

There isn't anyt any shortcut to turning into a skilled search engine optimization content material author.

you would love to exercise to come to be professional in search engine optimization content material writing.

The above-referred to talents if integrated via way of means of an search engine optimization article author then it is top for a enterprise that seeks expert offerings from the author . If you cherish to come to be an search engine optimization content material author then adhere to simple search engine optimization guidelines at the same time as writing content material and exercise hard.

SARA
JACKLINE

www.ingramcontent.com/pod-product-compliance
Ingram Content Group UK Ltd.
Pitfield, Milton Keynes, MK11 3LW, UK
UKHW061705190726
13853UKWH00008B/2419